Handmade

HOLIDAY CRAFTS

Handmade VALENTINE'S DAY Crafts

By Ruth Owen

Gareth Stevens
PUBLISHING

Please visit our website, www.garethstevens.com. For a free color catalog of all our high-quality books, call toll free 1-800-542-2595 or fax 1-877-542-2596.

Cataloging-in-Publication Data
Names: Owen, Ruth.
Title: Handmade Valentine's Day crafts / Ruth Owen.
Description: New York : Gareth Stevens Publishing, 2017. | Series: Handmade holiday crafts | Includes index.
Identifiers: ISBN 9781482460919 (pbk.) | ISBN 9781482461602 (library bound) | ISBN 9781482460926 (6 pack)
Subjects: LCSH: Valentine decorations--Juvenile literature. | Handicraft--Juvenile literature.
Classification: LCC TT900.V34 O84 2017 | DDC 745.594'1618--dc23

Published in 2017 by
Gareth Stevens Publishing
111 East 14th Street, Suite 349
New York, NY 10003

First Edition

Produced for Gareth Stevens Publishing by Ruby Tuesday Books Ltd
Designer: Emma Randall

Photo Credits: Courtesy of Ruby Tuesday Books and Shutterstock.

Printed in the United States of America
CPSIA compliance information: Batch CW17GS:
For further information contact Gareth Stevens, New York, New York at 1-800-542-2595.

CONTENTS

A HAPPY HANDMADE HOLIDAY

When February comes around, the shops are filled with beautiful—but sometimes expensive—cards, decorations, and Valentine's gifts.

This year, try the projects in this book and you'll soon be creating your own Valentine's Day celebration using inexpensive crafting supplies and scraps of **recycled** materials from around your home.

All you need to do is follow the instructions, throw in a little of your own **creativity**, and you'll soon be having a very happy handmade holiday!

STAY SAFE

It's very important to have an adult around whenever you do any of the following tasks:

- Use scissors
- Use a knife
- Use wire cutters
- Use a glue gun

YOU WILL NEED:

To make the projects in this book, you don't need any special equipment—just some basic crafting tools and supplies.

• Scissors
• Duct tape
• Glue gun
• White glue
• Paints and paintbrushes
• Tape
• Stapler
• Wire cutters

GLITTER ROSE VALENTINE'S CARD

It wouldn't be Valentine's Day without giving cards. This easy-to-make rose design looks impressive, but is simple to make using celery as a **stamp!**

YOU WILL NEED:

- A bunch of celery
- A knife and cutting board
- Thin card stock in your choice of colors
- A saucer
- Paint
- Glitter
- Scissors
- White glue
- Colored markers

1 Ask an adult to help you cut off the base of the bunch of celery. You will use this as your stamp.

2 Put some paint into the saucer.

3 Dip the cut ends of the celery into the paint and make sure each stalk is well covered with paint.

4 Now firmly press the celery onto the card stock to create a rose shape.

5 While the paint is still wet, sprinkle with glitter. Then shake off any excess glitter.

6 When the rose is dry, cut it out.

7 Now fold a piece of card stock in half to create a greeting card and glue the glitter rose to the front.

8 Use the markers to write a Valentine's greeting on the front of the card.

Be My ...

... Valentine!

HEART PAPER CHAINS

When your Valentine's Day cards are made, get busy creating decorations for the big day, such as these heart paper chains.

YOU WILL NEED:

- Colored paper
- Scissors
- Stapler and staples

1 Begin by cutting the paper into strips that measure about ¾ inch (2 cm) by 7 inches (18 cm).

2 Fold the first strip in half and then staple just above the fold.

3 Bend the two ends of the paper strip around, allowing the stapled crease to form the top indent of the heart. Staple the ends together.

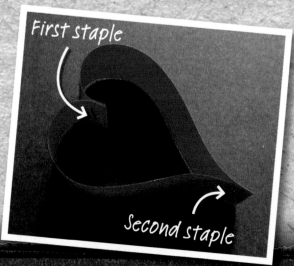

First staple

Second staple

4 Now fold a second paper strip in half. Staple the fold to the bottom of the first heart you made.

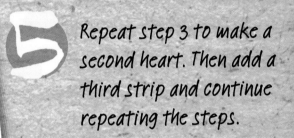

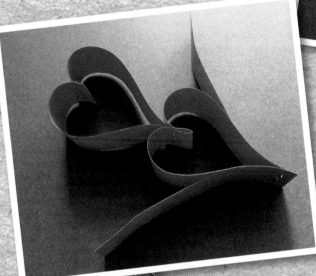

5 Repeat step 3 to make a second heart. Then add a third strip and continue repeating the steps.

You can recycle scraps of craft paper, magazines, or gift wrapping paper to make your heart paper chains.

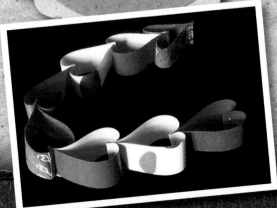

WOVEN HEART

A heart is the most **traditional** and popular **symbol** of love, and these cute card hearts will look great decorating your home or classroom for Valentine's Day.

YOU WILL NEED:

- Thin white card stock
- Thin red card stock
- Small bowl or saucer with a diameter of about 4.5 inches (11 cm)
- Pencil
- Scissors
- Tape

1 Cut a piece of white card stock that's 7 inches by 4.5 inches (18 x 11 cm).

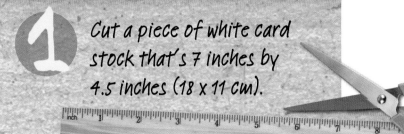

2 Place an upturned saucer or bowl on one end of the card stock, and draw around the right-hand side of it to create a rounded end for the rectangle of card stock.

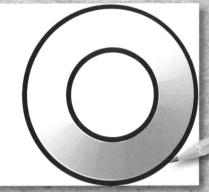

3 Repeat steps 1 and 2 with a red piece of card stock.

4 Cut out the curved end of each piece of card stock.

Straight end

Curved end

Now cut three slots in each piece of card stock. Cut from the straight end toward the curved end, and stop cutting just where the curve begins.

6 The two halves of your heart are now ready to be woven together, as shown.

1. Top white strip tucks under the top red strip.

2. Then the white strip slides over the red strip.

3. White strip slides under the red strip.

4. Then the white strip slides over the top of the red strip.

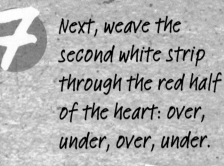

7 Next, weave the second white strip through the red half of the heart: over, under, over, under.

8 Then weave the third white strip: under, over, under, over.

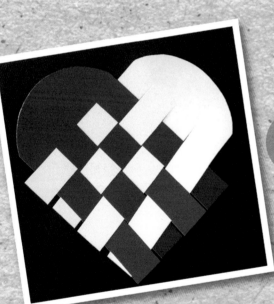

9 And finally weave the fourth white strip into the heart.

10 Once all the strips are woven together, tuck the ends of the strips behind the model and secure them with tape.

RECYCLED MAGAZINE HEARTS

If you've got some old, glossy magazines, you can recycle them into funky, heart-shaped Valentine's decorations.

YOU WILL NEED:

- A thick, glossy magazine
- Marker
- Scissors
- String or ribbon

Make sure you choose a magazine with thick, glossy pages and a thick spine that's glued—not a spine that's held together with staples.

paper

paper

Thick, glued spine

1 Lay the magazine flat on a surface with the open pages toward you and the spine away from you.

Spine

MAGAZINE COVER

Open pages

Spine

folded cover

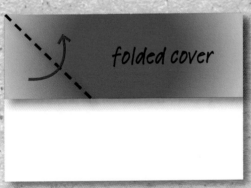

2 Now fold the magazine's cover in half away from you and toward the spine, and crease well.

3 Fold up the left-hand corner of the cover along the dotted line, and crease well.

folded cover

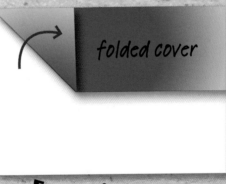

folded cover

Open pages

Page 1

Spine

4 Then open out the folded cover so it's flat against your work surface.

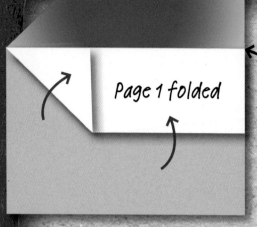

Page 1 folded

Spine

5 Repeat steps 2 to 4 with the next page (or first inside page) of the magazine. Fold the page in half toward the spine, fold up the left-hand corner, and then fold over the page so it's on top of the cover that you've already folded.

6 Now repeat with all the pages of the magazine.

When all the magazine's pages are folded, it should look like this.

Open pages

Spine

7 Lay the magazine flat on a surface with the spine to the right. Draw a semicircle on the cover with a marker.

Spine

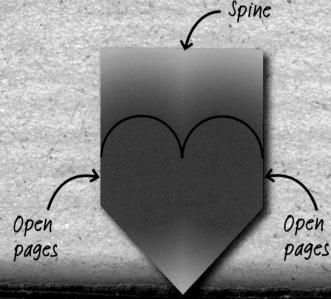

Open pages

Open pages

8 Open out the magazine and lay it flat. Draw a mirror image of the semicircle on the other side of the spine.

Throw away

Cut here

9 Now, working with a few pages at a time, cut along the lines you've just drawn.

To remove the pages completely, tear them from the spine.

10 When you've cut and torn off all the pages, the magazine will look like this.

Cut off the spine "stalk" that's left behind.

Spine stalk

11 Now find the heart's 12 center pages. Fold down and crease the top, curved edge of each of these pages.

Folded center pages

12 Thread a piece of ribbon or string around the center of the heart.

Then hang up the heart with the back of the decoration against a wall or other flat surface.

VALENTINE'S GLITTER GLOBE

Nothing says "I Love You" like a beautiful handmade gift. So try making these mini glitter globes to give to the special people in your life.

YOU WILL NEED:

To make one globe
- Small glass jar with an airtight lid
- Small styrofoam ball that fits inside the jar
- A small knife
- A pipe cleaner
- Scissors
- Glue gun
- A teaspoon
- Pure glycerin
- Water
- Glitter
- Red paint or ribbon

1 Ask an adult to help you cut about one third from the styrofoam ball.

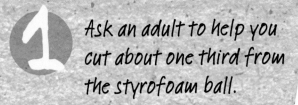

2 Twist a pipe cleaner into a small heart that will fit inside the jar.

Shape the heart and pinch here.

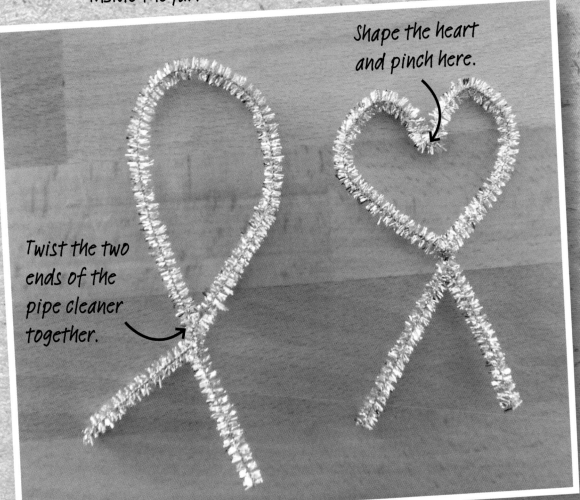

Twist the two ends of the pipe cleaner together.

3 Take hold of the larger piece of styrofoam ball. Ask an adult to help you cut a slot through the styrofoam.

4 Push the ends of the pipe cleaner heart through the slot in the ball, so the heart sits on the ball. Then trim off the ends.

5 If you wish, you can paint the jar lid red or another color.

6 Using the glue gun, stick the styrofoam ball inside the lid of the jar.

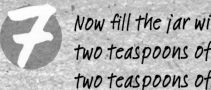 Now fill the jar with water. Add two teaspoons of glycerin and two teaspoons of glitter—or more glitter if you'd like! Stir well.

The glycerin makes the water more **viscous** so it takes the glitter longer to settle in the globe.

8 Carefully lower the heart into the jar and tightly screw on the lid. If you wish, you can add a red ribbon around the jar.

Tip the jar upside down, give it a shake, and your glitter globe is ready to give!

23

FABRIC SCRAP HEARTS

These fabric hearts can be made into a brooch or barrette, or simply given as a **unique**, handmade Valentine's gift.

YOU WILL NEED:

- A glass
- A marker or pencil
- Red felt plus colored scraps for decoration
- Colored fabrics
- Scissors
- Glue gun
- Buttons
- Hair clips or safety pins

1 Begin by cutting out a circle of red felt, and nine circles in your choice of fabric. To make a circle, place a glass upside down on the reverse side of the fabric and draw around it with a pencil.

2 Cut out the circles.

To give our fabric a **crinkly** edge, we used pinking shears.

3 To create a heart base, fold the red felt circle in half. Then make cuts along the lines as shown.

When you unfold the felt circle, you will have a heart.

4 Take a fabric circle and fold it in half. Then fold in the left-hand half of the semicircle and hold it in place with hot glue.

5 Fold in the right-hand side of the semicircle and glue in place, so you have a small cone. Repeat with the other eight fabric circles.

6 Now you are ready to assemble your heart. Glue the fabric cones to the heart base as shown.

First cone in place

Four cones glued in place

Keep adding cones until the heart base is covered. Now you can add decorations to the heart.

7 To complete our design, we cut out a small red and purple heart and glued them in the center. Then we added a pearly button.

8 To make a brooch, carefully thread a safety pin onto the back of the heart. To make a barrette, glue or stitch a hair clip to the back.

EASY YARN HEARTS

Get winding with yarn to make this fun Valentine's decoration or gift.

YOU WILL NEED:

- Thick, stiff wire or a wire coat hanger
- Duct tape
- Wire cutters
- Yarn in your choice of color
- Scissors

1 Begin by making a heart shape in stiff, thick wire. Ask an adult to help you bend and cut the wire.

2 Secure and wrap any cut ends of wire with duct tape.

3 Tie the yarn to the wire frame with a double knot and then get winding.

Wind the yarn around the wire frame twice and pull tight.

Tie the yarn to the wire heart here.

4 Keep winding the yarn around the frame. Wind in and out of the frame, too.

Open heart

5 Stop winding when you like the look of your design and tie off the yarn in a double knot. Tie a piece of yarn to the frame so you can hang up your heart.

Filled-in heart

You can either make an open design or completely cover the frame with yarn to make a filled-in heart.

GLOSSARY

creativity
The use of imagination or original ideas to create something new and unusual.

crinkly
Wavy or wrinkly.

recycled
Turning objects or materials into something new instead of throwing them away.

stamp
An object in a particular shape or engraved with a design that is dipped in paint or ink and used to impress a pattern onto paper, fabric, or other materials.

symbol
An object or picture that stands for, or represents, another thing. For example, a heart shape is a symbol that represents love.

traditional
A way of thinking, behaving, or doing something that a group of people have followed for a long time. For example, decorating our homes with hearts and other red decorations is part of our traditional Valentine's Day celebrations.

unique
Something that is one of a kind. Handmade objects are unique because each one is different from the next, unlike objects made in a factory.

viscous
Having a thick, sticky consistency.

INDEX

FURTHER INFORMATION

BOOKS:

Eick, Jean. *Valentine's Day Crafts.* Mankato, MN: RiverStream Publishing, 2012.

Ross, Kathy. *All New Crafts for Valentine's Day.* Minneapolis, MN: Millbrook Press, 2011.

WEBSITES:

http://www.activityvillage.co.uk/valentines-day-crafts
Find more handmade Valentine's Day crafts here.